Text and illustration copyright © 2018, 2020 by Chris Ferrie

Cover and internal design © 2020 by Sourcebooks

Cover and internal design by Will Riley

Sourcebooks and the colophon are registered trademarks of Sourcebooks.

All rights reserved.

Published by Sourcebooks eXplore, an imprint of Sourcebooks Kids

P.O. Box 4410, Naperville, Illinois 60567–4410

(630) 961-3900

sourcebookskids.com

First published as Red Kangaroo's Thousands Physics Whys: *All the Time in the World: Special Relativity*

in 2018 in China by China Children's Press and Publication Group.

Library of Congress Cataloging-in-Publication Data is on file with the publisher.

Source of Production: PrintPlus Limited, Shenzhen, Guangdong Province, China

Date of Production: April 2020

Run Number: 5018389

Printed and bound in China.

PP 10 9 8 7 6 5 4 3 2 1

# Let's Race!

## Sprinting into the Science of Light Speed with Special Relativity

sourcebooks
eXplore

**#1 Bestselling
Science Author for Kids
Chris Ferrie**

Red Kangaroo has been spending the morning doing her chores. "Finishing my chores is taking such a long time," she says.

But time always goes much more quickly whenever Red Kangaroo is playing and having fun. She wonders why. "I should ask Dr. Chris!"

"Hi, Dr. Chris! Can you tell me why time moves faster when I'm playing but moves so slowly when I'm doing my chores?" Red Kangaroo asks.

"It's actually just a trick of your mind!" Dr. Chris replies. "But it is a good example to help us learn all about special relativity!"

"What's that, Dr. Chris?"

"Special relativity is a theory that the famous physicist Albert Einstein discovered," says Dr. Chris. "The theory explains how space and time are connected. There are two ideas that make up this theory."

"The first idea is that the rules of physics are always the same everywhere in the universe. They don't change even if you are moving."

"That's easy to remember!" says Red Kangaroo. "If I'm on Earth or in space, I don't need to learn new physics!"

"The second idea is that the speed of light stays the same everywhere in the universe," Dr. Chris says. "Light moves very fast, and it is impossible for us to ever catch up with it."

"So the rules of physics never change, and light moves fast all the time. Got it!" says Red Kangaroo. "But what do those ideas have to do with special relativity?"

Light

"Have you ever been silly and tried to walk up escalator stairs that were moving down?" Dr. Chris asks.

"Yes! I tried going very fast but still didn't get very far," Red Kangaroo replies.

"That's an example of relativity!" Dr. Chris says. "To you it seemed like you were going up the stairs as fast as you could. But to everyone else you would look like you weren't moving at all!

"I think I get it!" Red Kangaroo says. "Movement can look different depending on your perspective."

"That's right," Dr. Chris says. "And Einstein used the two rules of special relativity to show that time and space can also be relative. He said they can stretch and squish."

"I've never seen time or space stretch or squish!"
Red Kangaroo says.

"That's because only very fast or very heavy things
notice when space or time squishes or stretches,"
Dr. Chris says. "We are not fast or heavy!"

"Speak for yourself, Dr. Chris! I am very fast!"
Red Kangaroo shouts.

"True! But nothing can travel faster than light!" Dr. Chris says. "The speed of light is the fastest speed in the universe. Light travels around the Earth seven and a half times in one second! Even in the fastest jet plane, it would take you about twelve hours to travel around the Earth once!"

"Whoa, that's fast! Time must be really squished for light!" says Red Kangaroo.

"If I tried my hardest, could I go as fast as light?" asks Red Kangaroo. "Sorry, it is impossible for us to go as fast as light moves," Dr. Chris says. "We have to use more and more energy the faster we go. It would feel like you were getting heavier and heavier!"

"So why doesn't light get heavier when it moves so fast?" Red Kangaroo asks.

"Light doesn't need energy to move because it is energy!" Dr. Chris says. "Light has no mass or weight. It never stops moving and is always going at the same speed."

"Wow! Light has a very different perspective of the world than we do!" says Red Kangaroo.

"It definitely does!" Dr. Chis replies. "Both time and space are really squished when you move as fast as light!"

"I really want to see time and space squish!" says Red Kangaroo. "Could I go as fast as light in a spaceship?"

"You certainly could try!" Dr. Chris says. "But don't forget about special relativity! The distance from Earth to other galaxies looks very far to us. But it will seem shorter to you in your fast spaceship."

"My measurement of the distance will be different from yours," Red Kangaroo says. "That's relativity!"

"That's right," Dr. Chris says. "And moving fast also means that the time it will take you to make the trip will feel shorter to you than it will feel to us on Earth."

"Great! If I travel close to the speed of light, then I can be home in time for dinner!" Red Kangaroo says as she waves goodbye and boards the spaceship. "See you soon, Dr. Chris!"

"I don't think Red Kangaroo quite understands special relativity yet," says Dr. Chris. "Time and space will squish for her when she travels closer to the speed of light. But they will feel very stretched out for us on Earth. "Soon" to her may mean many years for us!"

Dr. Chris

Within just a few hours, Red Kangaroo travels to the next galaxy and returns!

"I'm back, Dr. Chris!" she says. "I told you I'd be quick!"

But it hasn't been a few hours for Dr. Chris.

"Many years have passed here on Earth while you were away, Red Kangaroo!" Dr. Chris says. "I told you that time and space were relative!"

Now Red Kangaroo thinks differently about time when she does her chores. "Einstein's theory of special relativity taught me that time moves slowly when I try to move fast. I guess I should just slow down and try to enjoy my work!"

# Glossary

## Light
Pure energy with no mass that moves through space at 671 million miles per hour!

## Albert Einstein
## 1879-1955
A German scientist who created many theories of physics, including relativity and quantum physics.

## Mass
How much "stuff" is in a body. Something with more mass needs more energy to move.

## Physics
The science of mass, space, and time, and how energy and forces connect them.

## Space
The three dimensions in which all things exist and move.

## Special Relativity

A theory of physics that relates space to time (together called space-time). It explains how space-time is relative or looks differently based on the perspective.

## Time

The flow of events from past to present to future. We generally use clocks to measure time.

# Show What You Know

1. Name the two things that always stay the same based on the theory of special relativity.

2. Define what it means for something to be relative.

3. Dr. Chris used running up the "down" escalator as an example of relativity. Can you come up with another example of something that can appear funny with relative motion?

4. Name something that appears or feels different when we try to move very fast.

5. Does Einstein's theory of relativity really explain why Red Kangaroo thought time moved slowly when she did chores but moved quickly when she was having fun?

Answers on the last page.

# Test It Out

## Can you measure the speed of light?

1. You'll need a microwave-safe plate, a ruler, a bar of chocolate, a calculator, and a microwave.

2. Remove the turntable from the microwave and replace it with the plate. Make sure the plate is upside down.

3. Put the chocolate on top of the plate and heat it until it melts in two or three places. (This will probably take about twenty seconds.) Be safe and ask an adult for help!

4. Take the chocolate out of the microwave and use the ruler to measure the distance between the melted spots.

5. It's time for some math! Multiply the distance between the melted spots by two.

6. Now multiply that number by 2,450,000,000. (Note: Check inside or on the back of your microwave for a label that says 2,450 MHz. If has a different MHz number, you need to multiply by that number instead.) This is the number of times per second that light waves are moving up and down in a standard microwave.

   Check to see if any of your answers are close to the speed of light! (Light travels 11,802,852,677 inches per second or 29,979,245,800 cm per second.)

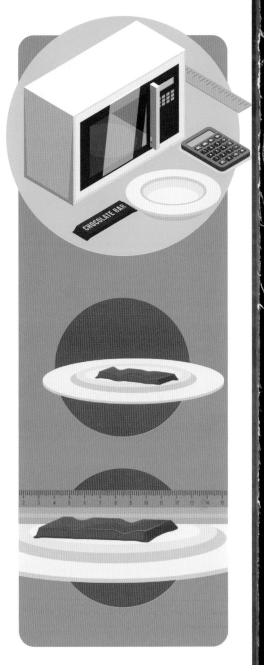

# Ball in motion

1. You'll need a friend, a ball, and a skateboard or skates. (If you don't have either, you can just walk or run—you just need a way to be in motion.)

2. One person will need to be the Observer. The other person will be the Performer.

3. The Performer will skate back and forth on the sidewalk or some other flat surface. While they are moving, they will also throw the ball up and catch it as often as they can.

4. The Observer will stand in one spot and watch the Performer skate by them.

5. Both the Performer and the Observer should watch the ball as it is being tossed and caught. Describe the motion of the ball from your point of view. What path does the ball take as it is tossed and caught?

   Compare what you each noticed about the ball's motion. Did you both see the ball moving in the same way or did the ball move differently depending on your perspective?

# What to expect when you Test It Out

## Can you measure the speed of light?

When you measure the distance between two of the melted spots, you got the half wavelength of the microwaves. We multiplied it by two to get a full wavelength. The frequency (the number of times the waves move up and down in a second) was 2.45 billion per second. Once per second is a Hertz. So, your microwave uses light with frequency 2,450 million Hertz, or 2,450 MHz. The formula to measure speed is wavelength times frequency. Microwaves produce electromagnetic waves with frequency in the microwave region of the electromagnetic spectrum. This is light that your eyes cannot see. This also means they travel at the speed of light!

## Ball in motion

The Performer will see the ball go straight up and straight down into their hand. The Observer will see the ball go up and down as well, but it will also move to the side along with the Performer. Two perspectives, two different paths for the ball. Which is correct? They both are! That's relativity. By the way, the Observer will notice that the ball moves not in straight lines, but in an arc. This is because the ball has mass and is being pulled by the force of gravity. If the ball were a beam of light, it would move in a straight line from all points of view.

# Show What You Know answers

1. The rules of physics and the speed of light are the same for all observers.

2. Things are relative when they can look or be experienced in different ways based on different perspectives.

3. Any situation where two things are moving at different speeds works here! How about